Leading into the 21st Century...and Beyond! 2.0

David Spell

Leading into the 21st Century…and Beyond: 2.0 by David Spell Copyright ©2016 by DavidSpell.com All Rights Reserved. Published in the United States by DavidSpell.com

Leading into the 21st Century…and Beyond was originally published in 2012. This new edition contains an updated and revised text plus many new chapters!

All photos are used under the Creative Commons License.

ISBN: 9781980536550

Table of Contents

Foreward
1. Defeat from Victory or Victory from Defeat?
2. How Long is Your Reach?
3. To Impress or Influence?
4. The Leader as a Follower
5. The Two Faces of Leadership
6. Leading from the Middle
7. Keeping Your People Sharp: Providing More Training
8. Where Does Authority Come From?
9. A Few Leadership Lessons from Bobby Cox
10. Leadership versus Management?
11. What Does it Take to Get Promoted?
12. Healthy Hearts, Healthy Lives
13. Loyalty or Leaving the Body in the Cave?
14. A Key to Learning and a Key to Leading
15. Josh's Big Mistake
16. Dealing with Fear
17. Blurry or High Definition
18. The Power of a Good Story
19. Who is Your Coach?
20. Without a Trace or Leaving a Mark?
21. Aaron and His Really Bad Day
22. Ingredients for Building a Great Team

23. The Stuff of Leadership
24. Who is the Greatest?
25. How is Your Vision?
26. Is Progress Always a Good Thing?
27. Management by Fear
28. Management by Fear- Part Two
29. Management by Involvement
30. How Did Jesus Develop Leaders?
31. The Unprotected City
32. Half Full or Half Empty?
33. Little Distractions or Big Dreams?
34. Getting Out of the Ditch
35. Good Decisions = a Good Life
36. A Season of Change- Setting Goals
37. A Season of Change- Writing it Down
38. Is There Ever a Perfect Time?
39. Leadership = Clarity
40. The Why of Leadership
41. Lessons Learned from Bad Bosses
42. Owning It
43. Always Learning
44. Losing it All
45. How Healthy is Your Team?
46. Keys to Reading More
47. Rabbi Jesus and His Band of Merry Men
48. Creating Culture
49. The Importance of Wisdom
50. Tips for Making a Major Life Change

Additional Books by David Spell

About the Author

Foreword

We are all affected by leadership, whether we like to contemplate that fact or not. None of us are truly independent and unless we are stranded by ourselves on a desert island in the middle of the Pacific Ocean, we all end up needing to be led or leading others at some time or other. Leadership can make our life better or worse, depending on the leader.

This book is a compilation of my own leadership journey over the last thirty plus years. I have been incredibly blessed to be helped along the way by some of the best. First of all, I have to mention my pastor for many years, Dean Sweetman, of the C3 Church. Dean is the best I have ever seen at raising up strong, independent thinking, and loyal leaders. As a leader, he created the atmosphere that together, there was nothing that we could not accomplish on our own and as a team.

I would also like to mention Assistant Chief Tom Savage (retired) of the Gwinnett County Police Department. Chief Savage was one of the most encouraging and positive people that I have ever worked with. I learned so much about how to lead and how to manage from him.

Chief Savage is very demanding but he created an atmosphere in which his people wanted to do their best and give one hundred percent. He was also the master of going out of his way to share an encouraging word to the front-line troops. While many of the "brass" get caught up doing other things and staying in the safe confines of their offices, Chief Savage was a cop's cop who loved to spend time with the troops.

My last mention is Lieutenant John Brady, also of the Gwinnett County Police Department (retired). When I got promoted to sergeant, John was the first lieutenant that I worked for. He had spent many years working in Internal Affairs and had just recently come back to the Uniform Division. He was an absolute delight to work for. He taught me the nuts and bolts of management, supervision, and leadership.

The most important thing that I learned from Lieutenant Brady was something that he told me on the first day that I reported to him as a rookie sergeant. "I am OCD about some things. I want our reports and paperwork to be done correctly. At the same time, never forget that our people always come first. Our people are our greatest resource. Take care of your people and they will take care of you." Thanks for such great advice, John. I always tried to follow it as a sergeant and as a lieutenant before my own retirement.

Leading into the 21st Century...and Beyond was first released in 2012. However, I was never really happy with how the book was formatted on Kindle. I have reformatted the manuscript and revised several of the chapters. I have also added a number of new chapters to this edition. I hope you enjoy it!

You will notice that most of the chapters are short, only one or two pages in length. This was done on purpose. I would love for this to be the type of book that is immediately actionable. Many of the chapters also include "Leadership Take Aways." These are questions designed to stimulate your thinking and to give you some ideas on how that particular chapter can be implemented.

David Spell
Curitiba, Brazil, 2016

Chapter One
Defeat from Victory or Victory from Defeat?

I have always been a bit of a Civil War history buff. A few years ago, I had the opportunity to tour the Shiloh Battlefield in Tennessee. It is a beautiful national park and one of the most well-preserved of all the Civil War Battlefields. This battle, at the time, marked the bloodiest single day and the bloodiest two days in American History. The Battle of Shiloh was important for many reasons, but one of the main keys to this battle, hinged on leadership.

General Albert Sidney Johnston was in overall command of the Southern forces. He was considered one of the brightest and most capable of all the Southern generals. General Johnston was able to achieve almost complete and total tactical surprise when his troops attacked the Federal forces, commanded by General U. S. Grant, on April 6, 1862. The Southern forces dominated the fighting and pushed the Union troops back throughout the day. The South was clearly winning the fight and had the North on the run. The Union forces were pushed back several miles to, where by the end of the day, their backs were up against the Tennessee River.

Around 2:00 in the afternoon, however, General Johnston was leading from the front as he often did. The general made an inviting target, though, and he was shot. General Johnston died shortly thereafter. Command of the Southern forces was passed on to General Beauregard, a much more cautious and a much less charismatic leader.

Throughout the day, Southern troops thinking that their victory was won, stopped fighting and took the time to loot the Federal camps that they had overrun. Discipline broke down and the officers lost control of their men. Instead of the Southern army continuing to press the beaten and broken Federals, they allowed them to catch their breath.

As the sun began to set and the day ended, one of General Grant's subordinate generals approached him. This general had seen the terrible beating that their army had suffered throughout the day. He asked Grant, "General, should I start boarding the men on the steamships for retreat?"

Grant quickly answered him, "Retreat? Hell, no! I plan on attacking them in the morning and defeating them!"

Grant had seen the exact same things that his subordinate had seen yet Grant also saw the possibility of still gaining victory from this apparent defeat. On the morning of April 7, Grant ordered his forces to counter-attack the Southern forces. This was the last thing that the Southern forces expected. The surprised Confederates fought hard but they had lost their advantage and were clearly losing this fight. By late in the afternoon, Grant's army had pushed Beauregard's army back and regained most of the ground that was lost the previous day. Southern Commander Beauregard, seeing the inevitable, ordered his forces to retreat.

General Grant was both criticized and praised for this battle. He was criticized because he allowed himself to be so totally surprised on the first day of the fight. He was praised because he was able to turn a defeat into a victory. This victory helped cement his reputation as a fighting general. Grant went on to eventually all of the Union forces to defeat the Confederacy.

Leadership Take Aways

1. We all have the ability to see the same facts. Often, however, it is our attitude that makes all of the difference in the battle.

2. Whether it is on the battlefield or in the boardroom, there is just no substitute for good leadership. People are looking to be led. Are we going to lead them to defeat or to victory?

3. Have you even been able to turn a situation around that looked like it was going to be a defeat?

Chapter Two

How Long is Your Reach?

"Good leaders influence their audience; great leaders influence the world." Michael Hyatt

Leadership equals influence. Leaders influence people. A question that I have been mulling over lately is, "How can I increase the reach of my influence?" Is that even possible? Can a leader enlarge their own leadership platform? Should this even be something that a leader should try and do?

For many leaders, this is not even a consideration. They are content with the sphere of influence that they have. They have no desire to increase the reach of their leadership. This is not necessarily a bad thing. When I worked for the police department, for example, I knew many great sergeants who did not want to get promoted to lieutenant. They were satisfied leading at that level and did not want to go any higher.

For many others leaders, however, you feel something stirring inside of you to reach farther and enlarge your platform so that you can help more people. You love influencing those around you, but you also want to have an impact on a larger scale. What would it take to make this happen for you?

If you are a pastor, this might mean starting a second service. It could mean opening a new campus or even planting a new church in another city or even another state. My home church has three campuses near Atlanta. They also have helped plant a number of other churches around the United States.

If you are businessperson, maybe this is the time to open a new location or look for new markets that have not been reached yet. If you have always thought about writing a book, maybe this could be the year that you get it on paper so you get your message out to a larger audience. One practical way that leaders can increase the size of their platform is by blogging. You may already have people that want to hear what you have to say. A blog could allow you to get your message to an even larger audience.

Leadership Take Aways

1. How big is your sphere of influence?

2. Are you content with it as it is or would you like to see it enlarged?

3. What are some ways that you have worked to increase your leadership reach?

4. What is one thing that you can do today to enlarge your reach?

Chapter Three

To Impress or to Influence?

"Don't be selfish; don't live to make a good impression on others. Be humble, thinking of others as better than yourself. Don't think only about your own affairs, but be interested in others, too, and what they are doing. Your attitude should be the same that Christ Jesus had." The Apostle Paul

"We can impress people from a distance but we can only influence them up close." Rick Warren

Leadership is influence. This can be good or bad. How are we influencing those around us?

We influence people when they can look us in the eye and decide that we can be trusted.

We influence people when we listen to them.

We influence people when we show them that we care about them.

We influence people when we acknowledge that we were wrong.

We influence people when we are open and honest about our own struggles.

We influence people when we allow ourselves to be vulnerable.

Leadership Take Aways

1. What are some other ways that we can influence people?

2. How have you been influenced your leaders?

Chapter Four

The Leader as a Follower?

"**Remember your leaders who taught you the Word of God. Think of all the good that has come from their lives, and follow their example of faith."**

I really enjoy reading, studying, writing, and teaching about leadership. I even enjoy actually leading! One aspect of leadership that is often overlooked, however, is that of following. If I do not follow well, I am probably not going to lead well.

At every level of leadership, there should always be someone that we are looking to for guidance, coaching, and accountability. One of the most important character qualities that effective leaders must have is that of humility. Humility allows us both to follow and to lead. In his excellent book, *Follow the Leader*, Simon McIntyre, pastor of C3 Church London, defines humility as, "being able to be told something about yourself or performance that requires correction or serious attention."

The person who views themselves only as a leader is missing out on valuable feedback that can only come when we are also a follower. Our subordinates are probably not going to point out our blind spots or areas that we need help in. Every leader needs a mentor, someone in a higher position, or who has greater experience than us. If we are going to lead well, we must also learn to follow well.

Leadership Take Aways

1. How are your "Followership" skills?

2. Who are you getting feedback from?

Chapter Five

The Two Faces of Leadership

"As apostles of Christ we certainly had a right to make some demands of you, but we were as gentle among you as a mother feeding and caring for her own children. We loved you so much that we gave you not only God's Good News but our own lives, too."

The Apostle Paul had founded the church in the city of Thessalonica on his second missionary journey. Persecution had forced Paul and his ministry partner, Silas, to leave town after just a few weeks. You can read the whole exciting story here. As soon as he could, Paul wrote the Thessalonian Christians a letter reminding them of the things that he had taught them. This letter also included some excellent insights into Paul's leadership style.

Here in First Thessalonians, Paul discusses the two faces of leadership. He says that when he was with the Thessalonians, he was as gentle "as a mother feeding and caring for her own children." The first face of leadership is that of a mother. There are many times when we need to be "mom" to people. This is especially true of new or weak Christians.

Paul said that he gently nurtured and fed the new believers. The picture here is of a nursing mother. She is feeding her baby from her own body. This requires her to be healthy and nourished herself. As leaders, we can only feed people if we are healthy ourselves. If we are not feeding ourselves on God's Word and spiritual food, we are not going to have anything to feed others with.

Mothers also convey a gentleness that fathers just cannot duplicate. Sometimes, Paul seems to be saying, the best thing that we can do as leaders is to give the person a hug or or a kind word to let them know that we believe in them. A good mom has a way of reassuring and comforting their child that lets them know everything is going to be okay.

In pointing out this first face of leadership, it is important to remember that this is not a male/female thing. Guy leaders also have to convey the "mom" side of leadership. Over and over again Paul tells leaders to lead with a spirit of gentleness.

The second face of leadership is that of a father. The father is often the one who brings discipline. Most of us have heard the words, "Just wait until your father gets home!" Discipline has negative connotations but in its purest form, discipline has to do with training. The word "disciple" comes from "discipline."

Discipline is a vital part of life. No athlete will ever become successful without discipline in their lives. No military force wins a battle unless they are disciplined. When a father correctly provides discipline for their children, they are providing guidelines for the child to follow.

Paul said later in the letter to the Thessalonians, "And you know that we treated each of you as a father treats his own children. We pleaded with you, encouraged you, and urged you to live your lives in a way that God would consider worthy. For he called you into his Kingdom to share his glory."

While dads can be gentle and nurturing, no one ever mistook their dad for their mom! Dads are probably going to be more direct with their children than mom is. Fathers usually have ways of motivating their kids that mothers just do not.

The "dad" face of leadership is the one that leaders will probably employ most of the time. This leadership style, done correctly, trains people, challenges people, motivates them, corrects them, and encourages them. Those whom we lead need both faces of leadership. Everyone can have a bad day when they need a mother to comfort and encourage them. Most of the time, though, we are going to set standards, implement guidelines, train, and encourage our followers to be the best that they can be.

Leadership Take Away

Which face of leadership do you relate to the most?

Chapter Six

Leading From the Middle

Most leadership books and seminars will, at some point, talk about the importance of Leading from the Front. In this chapter, we are going to talk about the neglected art of Leading from the Middle. If you are a middle manager, you probably do not get a lot of opportunities to lead from the front. The nature of your job is that you are often behind the scenes and out of sight. Leading from the middle is not nearly as sexy as leading from the front, but it is an extremely important role in any organization.

In most organizations, the front line supervisors are the driving force that makes things happen. Any military veteran will tell you that it is the senior non-commissioned officers, sergeants and chiefs that run the military. It is the front line supervisors that keep any organization moving forward. If an executive or manager needs something done, the best thing that they can do is entrust to a good front line supervisor.

So, if front line supervision is so crucial, what is the role of those in middle management? In many organizations, middle management is seen as the graveyard of aspirations. Middle managers are often required to work longer hours, attend monotonous meetings, deal with HR issues related to their subordinates, and always be available to their boss. While this does not sound like a glamorous job, those who learn to lead from the middle have the potential to influence the direction of their organization and the quality of the service that they provide for many years to come.

Why is middle management so important? Yes, it will be the CEO's, senior pastors, company presidents, and high ranking commissioned officers in the military that will set the vision for their organization, church, business, etc. It will be the middle managers, associate pastors, vice presidents, and lower ranking commissioned officers, however, who are going to make that vision a reality. They are going to make it happen by the way that they manage their front line supervisors.

The middle manager has the incredible opportunity to train,

mentor, and equip, and coach their front line supervisors. It is easy to overlook this in the day-to-day reporting of numbers, meetings with upper management, and other administrative responsibilities. While these things are important, there is nothing more important than our people. They are our most valuable resource. If we forget this important fact, we are treading on very thin ice.

There is nothing worse than a middle manager whose only interaction with their subordinates is to, "get those numbers for the CEO," or to ask, "What is holding things up on the line?" If we only talk to our front line supervisors when something is wrong or when we feel that we need to correct something, we are not doing them or our organization any favors.

The most effective middle managers are those who spend some time each day interacting with their subordinates. Instead of feeling that we should be telling them something, let's try getting into the habit of listening to their concerns and issues with their subordinates. What are some ways that we can make their jobs easier? Are there any obstacles that we can remove that would make their jobs easier?

When middle managers invest in training and developing their front line supervisors, they are investing in their organization for many years to come. We want our front line supervisors, no matter what their title, to be investing in their subordinates as well. The middle manager is often the person who trains the supervisors in how to train their subordinates. This creates a positive culture in the organization that will result continual growth and improvement on every level.

Leadership Take Aways

1. As a middle manager, what can you do to invest in your subordinates?

2. Who is the best middle manager that you ever worked for?

3. What was it that made them so good to work for?

Chapter Seven

Keeping Your People Sharp: Providing More Training

The best companies and businesses seem to be the ones that invest the most in their people. They often provide regular in-service training for their staff. This training can cover a variety of topics such as customer service, communication skills, computer skills, safety, ethics, and many other topics. There can also be specific skills taught to a sub-set of the organization. If a factory installed a new piece of equipment on the production line, for example, there would need to be training designed to educate those who would be using that particular machine.

Providing training and development opportunities to the employees at your company is very important for several reasons. First of all, it communicates that the administration and management team cares enough about their workers to provide additional opportunities for them to develop. This shows that company leadership understands the importance of investing in their people.

Most companies offer training for their employees during regular business hours. The workers are on the clock but not doing their regular job. This conveys the message that production can slow down for a few hours as the employees attend class.

In some companies, all the workers might be sent to the class over a period of a couple of days so that the business does not have to completely shut down. When employees see that their management cares enough to send them to some type of class, motivation is often improved throughout the company. Increased motivation leads to greater morale and job satisfaction.

A second reason that training and development opportunities are so important is that it keeps the team sharp. On-going training provides them with the latest technical, legal, and specialized skills that they need to do their jobs. This will increase efficiency and productivity in workers. If management is serious about productivity, periodic classes will ensure that their employees have the most up-to-date information to do their jobs effectively.

In-service training also serves to keep the team sharp in another way. By giving workers a break from their regular duties, even if it is only for a day or a few hours, they are allowing them to recalibrate and rest. Many people have jobs that are monotonous and tedious. When these workers attend a class, they are able to unwind and use a different part of their brain for a little while.

A third reason that on-going training opportunities are important is that they have been shown to reduce employee turnover by as much as 70%. While training is an investment by the company into its employees, regular training opportunities also serve to help the workers invest back into the company. Training often stimulates new ideas and creativity and give the employees a greater sense of ownership.

One last reason why it is so important for a company to provide training and development opportunities for their people is that it is an investment in the organization's future. Training opportunities will often be a way that management can identify those employees who appear to be leaders. Identifying people who could possibly fill supervisory and management roles down the road is important for any business.

The worst time to start looking for qualified people to promote is when you need them. It is much better to start the process of training and developing potential leaders before there is a need. Having an active list of candidates for promotion is something that any large business should maintain.

Companies and organizations should make training opportunities available throughout the year. Their people will benefit from it and the company will benefit from it. Some successful businesses have quarterly training sessions in which employees receive an hour or two of training on different topics. Other companies will set up classes twice a year, requiring workers to attend half-day sessions.

Besides required training, many organizations will also offer optional training that employees can request to attend. There is no doubt that training workers can be expensive. At the same time, successful organizations realize that they cannot afford not to train and develop their people.

Leadership Take Aways

1. What kind of training and employee development opportunities does your organization provide?

2. Do you feel that your organization does an adequate job of investing in the workers?

Chapter Eight

Where Does Authority Come From?

"Well done, my good servant!" his master replied. "Because you have been trustworthy in a very small matter, take charge of ten cities."

The Parable of the Talents parable that Jesus told in Matthew 25 cuts across the grain of our society. So many people want and expect authority to be given to them before they have proven themselves. Just having a degree in particular field does not mean that someone is an expert.

The Kingdom principle that we see here is that faithfulness with responsibility leads to authority. We will never be entrusted with true authority until we have shown that we can be responsible with whatever tasks we are given. Learning to faithfully serve someone else's vision is a prerequisite for God entrusting us with our own vision.

Work hard and serve where you are planted. That work and service will produce the seeds for your future growth! Don't expect authority to be just given to you. Real authority comes to those who prove that they can handle it.

Leadership Take Aways

1. Have you ever known someone who was given too much authority before they were ready for it?

2. How did that work out for them?

Chapter Nine

Leadership Lessons from Bobby Cox

Former Atlanta Braves Baseball manager Bobby Cox was honored a few years ago by having his number retired and by being inducted into the Braves Hall of Fame. He was also a first round pick for the Baseball Hall of Fame in 2014. He is ranked number four on the all-time wins list by a manager with 2,504, and he led the Braves to fourteen division titles and to a World Series Championship in 1995.

It is always interesting to listen to what others say about someone that they have worked/played for. Longtime Braves infielder and future Hall of Famer himself, Chipper Jones, said, "He took a chance on me by drafting me. I have spent the last twenty years trying to make him proud."

Outfielder Jason Heyward came up through the Braves minor league system. During the one year that he played for Bobby, Jason said, "He treated me like I was part of the family. He included me in his thought process and explained things to me when he really did not have to." Here are a few of the leadership nuggets that are so apparent in the Bobby Cox Legacy.

1. He picked the right players.

Along with help from the scouts and the management team, Bobby consistently fielded a team of incredibly talented athletes. Picking winners was always a team effort. In many cases, this was rough, unpolished talent that would be developed in Atlanta's excellent minor league system. Jason Hayward and Chipper Jones are both excellent examples of this. There were certain attributes, though, which Bobby Cox always looked for, such as drive, determination, and quality of character to go along with their talent.

2. He picked a certain type of player.

There have been many talented players that Bobby and his staff passed on because they would not be a good fit in Atlanta. With rare exceptions, players that brought attention to themselves, players that complained to the press, and players who had discipline problems off the field were not going to last on a Bobby Cox team. The Atlanta Braves teams have had very good chemistry over the last

20+ years because Bobby and his scouts picked players that had the kind of chemistry that they were looking for. These great teams did not happen by accident.

3. He did not over manage.

After Bobby had put his team together, he let them play. If a guy was struggling to hit, or a pitcher was struggling to find the strike zone, Bobby was incredibly patient about letting them work their way out of the slump. He was often criticized by the baseball press for being too patient. His record of success speaks for itself.

4. He demonstrated loyalty to his players.

I have heard him in interviews being questioned about why the slumping or struggling player was still in the lineup. Bobby was always positive and optimistic. He would say, "He is a great player who is just going through a little rough stretch. It is just a matter of time before he breaks out of it." This loyalty was so appreciated by his players and they gave it back to him.

5. He took up for his players.

One of the all-time records that Bobby Cox holds is for being ejected from baseball games. This was before the days of instant replay. If an umpire missed a call, it was not uncommon for the player and/or the manager to challenge it in a loud and vocal manner! The thing that puts this record into context is the fact that most of the ejections have come while he was defending one of his players and trying to keep them from getting ejected from the game.

6. He always seemed to get the most out of his teams.

There were many years when the Braves did not have the most talented players in the league. Over the course of the 162 game season, though, most of the teams that Bobby managed won more games than they lost. As a manager, Cox instilled a culture of winning. He put that deep into the DNA of his teams so that year after year, they just seemed to find ways to win.

Leadership Take Aways

1. Leadership lessons and principles seem to make more sense when they are examined in a real flesh and blood leader.

2. Have you had a coach or other leader that was able to get more out of you than you thought you were able to give?

3. Have you ever played for or worked for someone who saw talent and potential in you that you did not even see yourself?

Chapter Ten

Leadership vs. Management

Is there a relationship between Management and Leadership? How closely are they related? In their most basic forms, Management has to do with control, while Leadership has to do with empowerment and release. Can these two ever work together?

While it is possible for managers to be leaders and for leaders to be managers, their functions are very different. Leaders cast vision, set the course, and point the organization in the way that it needs to go. Managers then oversee the process of getting the organization from Point A to Point B. Managers make sure that the right resources are in place, both human and otherwise. They also make sure that the right systems are set up to ensure success.

There is always going to be a natural tension between leadership and management. Even though they are on the same bus, Mr. Leader is looking far down the road, while Mr. Manager is focused on keeping the bus moving forward and on the road. The tension that is created is not a bad thing.

Mr. Manager must always remember that the goal is not just to keep the bus moving. The goal is to get the organization to their destination. Mr. Leader must listen to Mr. Manager when he says that they need to stop the bus for gas or maintenance.

In a small organization, there is less of a need for multiple levels of management. As growth occurs, however, there will need to be management and oversight to make sure that growth and movement continue to take place in a healthy manner. When Mr. Leadership and Mr. Manager work together, there is not much that they cannot accomplish.

Chapter Eleven

What Does it Take to Get Promoted?

Getting a promotion at work is a very satisfying accomplishment. A promotion usually brings additional pay and benefits, added responsibility, increased visibility within the company or organization, and a sense of reaching an important personal goal. What are some of the ways that a person can make themselves more promotable?

1. How Committed are You?

One of the first things that management looks at when considering promoting someone into a supervisory or leadership position is their commitment to the company. Do they view their present position as a career or as a stepping-stone to getting a better position elsewhere? Do they get to work early? Are they willing to stay late to complete a project?

If the person is not committed to the company or the organization in their present position, it is unlikely that they will change if they get promoted to a position of leadership. A promotion does not make someone more committed. The person who gets to work a few minutes early and stays late, often attracts the attention of management. The person that is always willing to pitch in to assist with a project, even if it is not their responsibility, likewise catches management's eye.

2. How is Your Attitude?

Whether we like it or not, a person's attitude will often play a significant role in whether or not they get promoted. The person who is always negative, talking bad about fellow employees or the company, or who is always complaining is not likely to be someone that management is going to entrust with more responsibility. A supervisor or a manager who has a bad attitude is only going to create subordinates that also have bad attitudes.

On the other hand, the person that has a positive outlook, speaks highly of others, and has the ability to encourage their peers will attract the attention of upper management. This person will often be seen as someone desirable to have managing other people. People with positive attitudes are so rare, this one characteristic can go a long way in helping someone get promoted.

3. What are You Doing to Make Yourself More Promotable?

Another important factor that someone would want to consider in making themselves more promotable would be seeking out additional training. The employee who has taken the initiative to take extra classes in their particular field, or in the areas of management, leadership, or human resources will often find themselves getting promoted. Even if they have to pay for this additional training, it will likely turn out to be an investment that pays long-term dividends.

The employee who invests the time, money, and effort to go back to school or to attend a work-related seminar is putting themselves in an advantageous position. This type of initiative will often attract the attention of the management team. When a better position becomes available in the company, management knows they have already someone who has gotten the extra training to take that next step.

4. How is Your Relationship with Your Boss?

Making your boss look good is so important if you want them to support you in your quest to get promoted. If you make your boss' life miserable, it is unlikely that they are going to support or assist you as you work towards getting a better position in the company. If, however, you are constantly making your supervisor shine and helping them look good to their boss, they are probably going to go out of their way to help you in any way that they can.

A great way of getting your supervisor to help you is to ask them what areas that you can improve in or what skills you need to learn for a higher position in the company. Take their advice to heart and make the changes that they recommend. This shows that you are teachable and willing to learn new things.

Also, ask your supervisor for additional responsibility. So few people do this. This shows that you are willing to go above and beyond what is normally expected of you. This is another one of those things that attracts management's attention.

Obviously, there are no guarantees in life or in the corporate world where promotions are involved. There are, however, many ways in which a person can make themselves more promotable. The person who takes the time to implement some of these things into their life and career is setting themselves up for success. In life, the person that is most prepared is usually the one that comes out on top.

Leadership Take Aways

1. Can you think of any other tips that you would give someone who is seeking a promotion in their career?

2. Which of the four things above do you think is the most important?

Chapter Twelve

Healthy Hearts, Healthy Lives

"Guard your heart above all else, for it determines the course of your life."

According to the Center for Disease Control, heart disease is the leading cause of death in the United States. It accounts for 26% of all deaths. Yet, as serious and as dangerous as heart disease is, there are simple steps that we all can take to decrease our risk. Losing a few pounds and getting some exercise a few days a week will go a long way to keeping our physical hearts healthy. Working to lower our blood pressure and keeping our cholesterol under control are two more important aspects of preventing heart disease.

As important as it is to protect our physical heart, however, this verse from Proverbs is actually talking about our spiritual heart, the part of us that connects with God. Spiritual cardiovascular disease can be as deadly as natural heart disease. In a real sense, spiritual heart disease is even deadlier because it affects our relationship with God. Heart disease can kill us physically, but spiritual heart disease can have eternal consequences.

What are some ways that we can prevent spiritual cardiovascular disease?

1. Proper Diet.

Feeding ourselves on the right things goes a long way towards protecting our hearts. The Word of God should be part of our daily diet. Feeding ourselves on those life giving words will keep our hearts vibrant and healthy. We should limit our intake of unhealthy things, such as certain television shows or movies, gossip, or websites that are going to take our hearts away from God. It is also important that we are in a good church where we can hear God's Word preached and taught on a regular basis.

2. Exercise.

Serving others is a great spiritual exercise. There is something about helping people and actively giving ourselves away that helps keep our hearts healthy. Turning our focus outward from our own problems to helping others is an amazing spiritual exercise with eternal benefits! Depression has become epidemic in our society. Looking outwards and serving others is a great antidote to depression.

3. Prayer.

As we saw above, high blood pressure and high cholesterol were two of the enemies of a healthy heart that we mentioned. In the spiritual realm, worry and fear have the same effect on our hearts. Left unchecked, worry, fear, doubt, and their many companions will kill our relationship with God. Faith-filled prayer will drive those things away. The Apostle Paul said, "Don't worry about anything, but pray about everything."

Just as a leader needs to keep his physical heart healthy to handle the rigors and stress that their job produces, it is just as important that the leader not neglect their spiritual life. Taking care of our spiritual health is just as important, and in many ways more important, than only looking after our physical health. Let's make sure we guard our hearts.

Leadership Take Aways

1. What is the condition of your heart?

2. What is something that you can do today to increase your physical heart health? Your spiritual heart health?

Chapter Thirteen

Loyalty or Leaving the Body in the Cave?

"But David's conscience began bothering him because he had cut Saul's robe."

David had already been anointed as the next king of Israel. He had a word from God that he was going to be the one to replace Saul. At the moment, though, King Saul was intent on tracking David and his men down and killing them.

At a crucial moment, it looked like God had given King Saul into his hand. David and his men saw Saul and his soldiers coming and they hid in a large cave. When the King stopped and went into the cave to relieve himself, David's men encouraged him, "Look what God has done! He has given your enemy into your hand to do with as you see fit."

How easy it would have been to kill Saul in the darkness of that cave. David did not even have to do it himself. All he had to do was give the word and one of his men would have handled it for him. Maybe this really was God giving Saul and the throne over to David?

It would have been so easy to justify it:

1. David had been anointed as the next king of Israel. It was his destiny.

2. David also had to think about his men. Saul wanted to kill them as well.

3. Saul had given David's wife, Michal, to another man.

4. Saul had repeatedly lied to David and had personally tried to kill him on several occasions.

5. Saul had slaughtered an entire town that had provided assistance to David and his men.

At this crucial moment, however, David said, "I can't raise my hand against the Lord's anointed." He understood the fact that because God had placed Saul on the throne, it would have to be God who removed him from that throne. If David had taken the throne by violence, it is likely that his own story would have had a much different ending. He could have even ended up being killed by one of his men at some point when they were disgruntled.

David demonstrated amazing self-control, wisdom, and loyalty here. No, Saul did not deserve David's loyalty. This was an early example of the military maxim, "Salute the rank, not the man." The man might not have deserved David's loyalty or respect, but David still saw him as, "the Lord's anointed."

Leadership Take Aways

1. How are you at showing loyalty and respect to those God has placed over you, especially those who might not deserve it?

2. How important do you think loyalty is when we discuss leadership?

Chapter Fourteen

A Key to Learning and a Key to Leading

"Learning requires humility."

"Leading requires humility."

There are so many characteristics that have been put forth describing good leadership. Every book on leadership has a list of what that author thinks are the most important. Humility is one of those characteristics that should be on everybody's list.

The best leaders are always learning. Leaders are learners. They are always looking for that new way of doing something. They are always looking for new ways to be more productive. They are always looking for new ideas that they can adapt and implement to their situation. John Maxwell says, "Great talent is good, but great talent with a spirit of learning is better."

To be a learner, however, requires acknowledging that I do not know everything and I can always get better. I do not have it all together and there are probably areas in my leadership that could be improved upon. While this sounds obvious, we have all worked for or been around leaders who would never admit that they had a flaw or weakness in their leadership ability. These leaders would never admit that there was something that they did not know.

When a leader lacks humility, their growth as a leader stunted. They also tend to be insecure, close-minded to new ideas, and quick to shift the blame. Working with or for a leader like this is usually a very unpleasant experience!

Humility is one those keys that unlocks so many doors. Here are John Maxwell's four ways to develop a spirit or attitude of humility:

1. Don't think less of yourself, just think of yourself less.

2. Allow yourself to fail, but know it's not the end of the world when you do.

3. When mistakes are made, recognize the problem, solve it and

move forward with new knowledge.

4. Live with the mindset that there is always something to learn from everyone.

Can you think of any other ways to cultivate humility in your life and in your leadership?

Chapter Fifteen

Josh's Big Mistake

"Joshua recorded these things in the Book of the Law of God. As a reminder of their agreement, he took a huge stone and rolled it beneath the oak tree beside the Tabernacle of the LORD. Joshua said to all the people, "This stone has heard everything the LORD said to us. It will be a witness to testify against you if you go back on your word to God."

Josh had some big shoes to fill. Moses had been the man who had led the people out of slavery by going head-to-head with the Egyptian Pharaoh. Moses parted the Red Sea. He brought water out of a rock in the wilderness. Moses prayed in food for them as they wandered in the wilderness. Moses was one of those bigger than life figures.

Moses knew that he would not be around forever, though, and he prepared and trained his assistant, Joshua, to take charge after he was gone. It was Joshua who then led the Hebrews into the Promised Land. By all accounts, Joshua was a brave and a fearless leader. He led from the front during the military campaigns and provided good, solid leadership during his lifetime. Joshua guided the people into the land that God had promised them. He was a strong and stable leader in those early days of nationhood.

Josh made one large and glaring mistake, however. He did not raise up someone to take his place as Moses had done with him. This mistake had long and lasting implications for the Hebrews. At the end of his life, Joshua warned the people of what would happen if they turned away from the Lord. He even gave his famous, "Choose this day whom you will serve" speech. He then set up a rock altar as a reminder of the covenant between the people and their God.

After Joshua's death, the Twelve Tribes entered a dark time period known as the Period of the Judges. "After that generation died, another generation grew up who did not acknowledge the LORD or remember the mighty things he had done for Israel. Then the Israelites did what was evil in the LORD's sight and worshiped the images of Baal. They abandoned the LORD, the God of their ancestors, who had brought them out of Egypt. They chased after other gods, worshiping the gods of the people around them. And they angered the LORD."

By not training someone to take his place, Joshua left a leadership vacuum after he died. This vacuum led to the people doing evil. "Everyone did what was right in his own eyes." There was no one to provide guidance for the twelve tribes so they created their own standards of right and wrong.

It is easy to wonder what might have happened if instead of setting up a rock altar, Joshua had set up a leader who he had trained and mentored as Moses had done with him. The time of the Judges was one of the darkest and most depressing times of Israel's history. The Judges provided sporadic leadership but one gets the feeling that they were leading by default. Good leadership is no guarantee that the people would stay on the straight and narrow path. No leadership, however, is a recipe for disaster.

Leadership Take Aways

1. Who would you say has had the most influence on you as a leader?

2. Who are you currently mentoring?

Chapter Sixteen

Dealing with Fear

"Fear not."

I heard Pastor Mark Driscoll speak about fear a few years ago. He asked the question, "Who or what are we afraid of?" For many leaders, fear is a constant companion. For others, it just rears its ugly head from time to time. The stress that many of us face is caused by fear in one form or another. This might lead to sleeplessness, sickness, or depression.

When we were younger, we might have thought of fear as peer pressure. As we get older, we might think of it as people pleasing. Who are we trying to please?

Fear is vision without hope.

Fear is powerful, but not rational.

So, how do we get from fear, worry, anxiety, nervousness, or whatever other form it attacks us in to, "Fear not?" Throughout Scripture, God tells us to, "Fear not," or "Don't be afraid." In almost every case, though, He also says, "...for I am with you."

If we can really get this truth in our hearts and minds, that God is with us, fear will begin to lose its power. I heard someone say recently, "Worry is temporary atheism." It is easy to worry and let fear begin to infect our thoughts if we forget that God is with us.

I know circumstances and situations can be scary. I have to remind myself, however, that nothing can separate me from the love of God. He has promised that He causes all things to work for my good, because I love Him and am called according to His purpose.

I have never seen worry cause anything to change. Worrying does not cause any situation to get better. Faith, on the other hand, has the power to move mountains. A little faith in a Big God will accomplish amazing things!

Leadership Take Aways

1. Those of us who are in a leadership role can often find ourselves confronting fear.

2. How do you combat fear and worry?

3. How do you move past fear to doing what you know you should be doing?

Chapter Seventeen

Blurry or High Definition

"Moses was 120 years old when he died, yet his eyesight was clear, and he was as strong as ever."

A few years ago, I noticed that the print of everything I tried to read was getting smaller. I was squinting and moving the book in or out while trying to read it. For almost a year, I thought there was some kind of government conspiracy against me. "Why are they making the print on everything so small?"

Then I thought, "Maybe they're just using smaller font to save money."

One day I was walking through Walmart and I passed by the rack that held the reading glasses. On a whim, I plopped a pair on my nose and picked up a magazine. Wow! Everything was clear and in perfect focus! I could see again! Now, I never leave the house without my trusty reading glasses.

I think on a deeper level, as we get older, our spiritual vision can get out of focus. As we progress through life, there is a tendency to gravitate towards the comfortable, the familiar, and the safe ways of doing things. We avoid the risks that we might have taken when we were younger. While this may lead to a peaceful existence, I'm not sure that this is the plan God has for us.

It is important that we stay in step with what God is doing in every generation. It is not going to look the same as it did 20, 30, or 40 years ago when I was a younger man. If I am going to stay relevant as a leader, though, I am going to have to keep my spiritual reading glasses handy so that I can clearly see how the Holy Spirit is working today.

How is your vision?

Chapter Eighteen

The Power of a Good Story

"The Kingdom of Heaven is like..."

Over and over again, Jesus used simple, everyday stories to communicate eternal truths. In Matthew's Gospel, especially, Jesus tried to help his listeners get a glimpse of what God's Kingdom is like. He did this by sharing these parables. He did not wrap his truths up in religious or technical language. He used language that everyone could understand. Jesus tried to make complicated concepts clear by comparing them to something simple that His audience could relate to.

This is still a challenge for those of us who preach and teach today. Do we communicate in ways that our audience can understand or are we talking over their heads? This is complicated even more during those opportunities when we get to speak to non-Christians. Do we use words and concepts that non-Christians can relate to or do we fall back to speaking "Christianese?" We must always be careful of using language that only Christians can understand.

This is why storytelling is so important for communicators. The person who can tell a good story will never lack for an audience. When Jesus told parables, his hearers were on the edge of their seats waiting to hear what was going to happen next. Good stories convey content and principles in ways that our hearers will remember for a long time. Even those who have not become Christians yet will find themselves pulled along by powerful stories.

Leadership Take Aways

1. How are your communication skills?

2. How are your storytelling skills?

3. What is one thing you can do to improve your ability to tell a story?

Chapter Nineteen

Who is Your Coach?

"Honor those who are your leaders in the Lord's work. They work hard among you and give you spiritual guidance."

Have you thanked God for your leaders lately? Part of the Divine Plan is that we have people in our lives who are looking out for us and helping us to grow. I have talked to many Christians over the years who stumble over this.

"I love God but I don't need someone to tell me how to live."

"Who are they to suggest that I change the way that I am disciplining my kids?"

"Why does the pastor keep talking about money and telling me I need to be a giver?"

"It is none of my pastor's business if I am sleeping with my girlfriend."

Every world-class athlete has a coach. Every great leader has a mentor. People who are the most successful in life have someone who they bounce ideas off of.

Leadership Take Aways

1. Don't reject the coaching. Embrace it. Ask for it. Act on it.

2. Let's not let our insecurities keep us from hearing people who God has placed in our lives to help us.

3. Who do you listen to for advice?

Chapter Twenty

Without a Trace or Leaving a Mark?

"We're here to put a dent in the universe."

I don't know about you, but when I read those words something leaps inside me. I know Steve Jobs was talking about leaving a mark in the context of Apple's revolutionary technology. And he did. Half the families in the United States have at least one Apple product. But when I see those words, I can't help but to think of eternal things.

On another occasion, Steve Jobs was trying to woo the President of PepsiCo to come work for him in the early days of Apple's history. Jobs could see that the man was wavering. Should he leave his successful and prosperous career for the unknown?

Steve saw that the Pepsi president was having trouble making up his mind. It was then that Jobs delivered the knockout punch: "Do you want to spend the rest of your life selling sugared water or do you want a chance to change the world?" Needless to say, Steve Jobs got his man.

Apple has blessed us with some incredible tools and toys. In the end, however, only what is eternal will last. God has given His people the awesome responsibility of advancing His Kingdom here on earth. Every life changed by the power of God leaves a mark. Together, we can put a dent in the universe. In fact, that was God's plan all along.

Leadership Take Aways

1. What would it take for you to change the world?

2. How can you put a dent in your universe?

3. Who do you know personally that making an impact on the world?

Chapter Twenty-One

Aaron and His Really Bad Day

"Moses saw that the people were running wild and that Aaron had let them get out of control and so become a laughingstock to their enemies."

Moses had been on the mountain for forty days meeting with God and receiving the Law. Meanwhile, Aaron was left in charge. Rather than leading the people, however, Aaron facilitated their worship of a false god. This story of Moses and Aaron gives us a great contrast between a strong leader and a weak leader:

Aaron could not restrain the people. "You want an idol? Bring me some gold and I will make you one."

Moses was able to restrain God. After Moses prayed for the people, "the Lord changed His mind" about destroying them.

Aaron was concerned about doing what the people wanted.

Moses was more concerned about obeying God.

Aaron was quick to shift blame. When Moses confronted him, Aaron said, "Don't get so upset. You know how evil these people are."

Moses was quick to accept responsibility. Moses asked God to forgive the people for their sin and even prayed that if God would not forgive them that the Lord would kill him along with them.

Weak leaders can do tremendous damage to an organization. Aaron's weak leadership cost many of the Israelites their lives. It was Moses' leadership that righted the ship and stopped God's judgment.

Can you think of any other contrasting characteristics of weak and strong leaders?

Chapter Twenty-Two

Ingredients to Building a Great Team

When I was a sergeant with the police department, one of the jobs that I had was in Special Operations. I was offered command of a new unit in which I got build it from the ground up. I recruited some good young officers and within a few months, we were turning heads. My unit included two corporals, ten police officers, my secretary and me. There were some months that this small unit made more arrests and wrote more tickets than all of the officers in entire precincts.

Success brings its owns challenges, however. Our incredible success caused the police department's brass to reasonably assume that if we could do that well with a few officers, we could really make an impact if we had more officers. We went from being a small, quick-reacting unit, to a bigger, slower, more institutionalized section of the police department. They added another layer of management that changed the way that we worked. Even though we were bigger, our productivity began to slowly drop.

One of the reasons that we had been so successful was that I had a very specific formula that I used in selecting officers for the unit. When the unit got bigger, I did not have the final say in who was added to the team. I had input but there were several others who participated in the decision making process. Some of the officers that were subsequently added were not a good fit, really did not perform well and contributed to our numbers and effectiveness going down.

Here is the formula that I used in building my team. This formula will translate well in most organizations or companies.

1. Character.

I want team members that I can trust to do the right thing, not just do things right. I don't want to have to worry about what they are doing when I am not around. They were chosen because I knew their character or I was able to get good recommendations from other supervisors that I trusted.

2. Chemistry.

When I am putting a team together, I select people that I want to be around. There were a lot of talented, experienced officers that wanted to come work with us. In many cases, however, the chemistry just was not there. Workplace drama can be eliminated or reduced if we pay attention to this important ingredient in the hiring or selecting process. During our first two years, this new unit had very little interpersonal conflict. In fact, during my entire thirty-year career as a police officer, I don't think I ever saw a unit get along better and accomplish so much.

3. Competence.

Competence is important but I rank it last. Of course, there are certain skills and a baseline competence that is required for any position that you are hiring for. I will still take someone with good character and chemistry but who might not be quite as knowledgeable in the job. If the person is willing to work hard and willing to learn, we can work together.

When I was assembling my team in Special Operations, I looked for younger, less experienced officers. Other supervisors said I was crazy to not go after the guys or girls who had already proven themselves. What I looked for, though, was an officer who was highly motivated. If they were willing to work hard, I knew that I could train them and they would become competent sooner, rather than later.

Choosing younger officers with less experience also gave us the opportunity to train them the way that we wanted them trained. Less experience meant less bad stuff to unlearn. Our success proved that this approach worked. Many of those team members ended up taking big career steps later because of how well they had performed for me.

Obviously, there are many work situations in which you are given an existing team and have little or no input in who is on the team. That requires a whole different set of skills in molding them into an effective team of police officers, firefighters, church leaders, sales people, or engineers. Building a great team, however, is one of the things that define great leadership.

What are some other things that you look for in people when you are building a team?

Chapter Twenty-Three

The Stuff of Leadership

This is an excerpt from a block of instruction that I taught regularly in the Police Supervision Course. This three-week class was for all new corporals, sergeants, and civilian supervisors in the police department. Of course, they were taught the practical aspects of supervision but helping them to begin to think like leaders is such an important thing. A great discussion question in regards to leadership is this: What are some of the character traits of an effective leader?

1. Decisiveness.

Leaders make decisions. There is nothing worse than following an indecisive leader. Indecisiveness creates a feeling of uncertainty in their followers. People want to follow someone who knows where they are going.

Fear is what keeps people from making decisions. Caution is good and it is important to consider various options. There comes a time, however, when it is time to act. Make a decision! That is what leaders get paid to do.

2. Positive Attitude.

Attitude creates atmosphere. Leaders are responsible for the atmosphere of their organization, section, or team. Followers feed off of their leader's positive attitude. There seems to be a strong correlation between productivity and creativity in companies and organizations that have a positive, affirming, and encouraging atmosphere.

3. Consistency.

We have all had that boss whose mood and outlook fluctuated from day to day (or hour to hour!). It is not a good feeling going to work and wondering who we will be working for that day. Will it be Dr. Jekyll or Mr. Hyde? I think we owe it to our people to maintain some level of emotional consistency. The boss should not be the person known for their mood swings!

I only mentioned three character traits. Can you think of any more that define an effective leader?

Chapter Twenty-Four

Who is the Greatest?

"Whoever wants to be a leader among you must be your servant, and whoever wants to be first among you must be the slave of everyone else." Jesus

Years ago, I was working a plainclothes security detail in a volunteer capacity for a very large Christian conference. Part of my duties included escorting the speakers to the stage. I was a bit shocked at how some very well-known Christian leaders completely ignored me as I guided them from the back of the Georgia Dome to the platform. There was no, "Hello," "How ya doing?," "Thanks for being here," etc.

Now that I am older, I understand that they were probably just focused on the lecture that they were about to deliver. A lasting impression of that conference, though, was when I escorted Dr. Jack Hayford to the stage. Dr. Hayford is known throughout the world for his powerful preaching and teaching and has spoken to millions of people. He was a pastor for many years of a large church in Van Nuys, California.

What made such an impression on me as a young leader was the fact that Dr. Hayford made a point to stop, shake my hand, look me in the eye, and thank me for being there. I also noticed that that he had a kind word or comment for everyone that he encountered, both before and after he spoke. It was a small thing but it really impressed me. Here was someone who was not too busy or too distracted to take a moment to notice those who were busy serving. This is a great lesson for all of us, leaders or not. Do we have time to offer a kind word to the clerk in the convenience store or our waitress during our business lunch?

For those of us who are in management, do we take the time to chat for a few minutes with our employees? Have we taken the time to get to know a little about them? I know that we are all busy but we should never underestimate the importance of giving people a little "face time" with the boss. If we, as "the boss," take the time to serve our employees, we are creating an environment in which they will serve their co-workers and our customers.

Leadership Take Aways

1. Do you take the time to greet those who cannot do anything for you?

2. Who can you serve with a kind word today?

Chapter Twenty-Five

How is Your Vision?

"Leaders see what others do not."

What is it about leaders that set them apart from other people? There are probably several things, but one important attribute is that of vision, their ability to see further and to see more clearly than those around them. Good leaders are often described as "Visionary Leaders." This is not just referring to their ability to see where the organization is going or being able to predict future trends. What is it that leaders see?

1. Leaders can see the Big Picture.

This may seem obvious but there has to be someone who understands the macro picture. This also can apply to leaders at various levels within the organization. A Department Head needs to see the big picture for their department. A Shift Supervisor needs to see the big picture for their shift. Knowing where and how they fit into the organization is vital if they are going to accomplish their mission.

2. Leaders see potential problems before they develop.

Successful leadership avoids potential problems. We can always learn from our mistakes and good leaders understand that mistakes are going to occur. At the same time, they take steps to prevent big mistakes from happening. Proverbs says that, "A prudent person foresees danger and takes precautions." The most effective leaders will steer their team around potential minefields rather than plowing through and hoping that they don't get blown up.

3. Leaders see potential in others and know how to help them reach it.

The best leaders are those that are actively developing other leaders. Great leaders are not trying to get more followers. They are trying to create more leaders. They are constantly seeking to reproduce themselves. Strong leaders are secure and not intimidated by other strong leaders. Effective leaders are constantly mining for gold in those around them. They provide potential leaders with opportunities to learn, grow, and develop their own leadership skills.

Can you think of anything else that leaders see?

Chapter Twenty-Six

Is Progress Always a Good Thing?

"I don't know where I'm going, but I'm on my way." Carl Sandburg

"Watch the path of your feet and all your ways will be established." Solomon

We hear much talk in society about the importance of "progress." Politicians and leaders talk about the progress that we make under their enlightened leadership. Social leaders often refer to the progress that their group is making in a particular area. It often sounds like progress is an end, in and of itself.

I wonder, though, if it is possible to make progress while going in the wrong direction. I can drive fast in the opposite direction of where I live. I am making progress but I am not going to get to the place I need to get to.

This is a trap that individuals, groups, even nations can fall prey to. Is what we are calling "progress" really progress or are we just going fast in the wrong direction? Chesterton speaks of progress as moving towards moral ideals. If that is an accurate or even partially accurate understanding of what true progress is, how do we measure up?

We don't often hear discussion of moral standards or ideals very much today. If anyone should dare bring up such a subject, they are very quickly shut down as being out of touch with progressive thinking. N. T. Wright said, "Our problem is not that we have forgotten what the moral standards are. We have forgotten what a moral standard is."

Christians and ultimately the Church should be the ones who uphold and point to Biblical moral standards. Unfortunately, the Church has often approached this in a hateful and a judgmental way. Today, it seems that the Church has swung far to the other extreme of not wanting to make waves or create controversy by acknowledging that we still believe and hold to absolute moral standards.

Is there a true north? Are there absolute standards that God has established? Is it possible for the Church to point out the True Path, the only way to make genuine progress in a way that is loving, respectful, and sincere?

As he so often did, C. S. Lewis cut through the clutter of false ideas and ideologies: **"Progress means getting nearer to the place you want to be. And if you have taken a wrong turn, then to go forward does not get you any nearer. If you are on the wrong road, progress means doing an about-turn and walking back to the right road; and in that case the man who turns back soonest is the most progressive man."**

Chapter Twenty-Seven

Management by Fear

If you are in management or know anything about management, you are probably familiar with the terms Management by Objectives (MBO), Management by Consultation (MBC), Management by Strengths (MBS), or Management by Walking Around (MBWA). These terms provide managers with strategies to help them manage effectively. In reality, most managers use different strategies depending on what needs to get accomplished.

One style that we don't often hear about, yet is too often alive and well, is Management by Fear (MBF). I have seen this style used in the police department, in the corporate world, and even in the Church. In this style, managers use fear and intimidation to control their workers and attempt to make them perform better.

Several years ago, a large department store at a mall hired a number of us local police officers to work security there to curb shoplifting. It was an easy job for us and paid well. It also provided me with a unique position to observe how the store was managed. The store manager, George, used Management by Fear as his only management style. I don't think he knew any others. This had the trickle-down effect. Most of his assistant managers utilized the same style.

I would be standing in an area talking to a sales clerk and

watching people shop. We would hear George coming because his shoes clicked on the tile floor. The clerk would whisper, "George is coming," and start acting busy, folding shirts or rearranging a display. George would appear, point to several clothes racks or displays that looked good already, and then order the clerk to straighten them. He would then stomp over to the next department and repeat his performance.

This was the only time the employees saw George. His conversations were short, one-way, and unfriendly. I understand that Management by Walking Around (MBWA) is a great way to find out what is going on in the workplace, but this was more like Walking Around and Looking for Something to Criticize.

Leadership Take Aways

1. Have you ever worked for someone like this?

2. Why do you think some managers feel like fear is their only way to motivate workers?

3. Do you feel that fear is a good way to motivate people in the workplace?

Chapter Twenty-Eight

Management by Fear: Part Two

The results of Management by Fear are all bad. First of all, if the store manager, senior manager, senior pastor, CEO, etc., uses this style, their associate managers will probably adopt it as well. In the department store that I referred to in Part One most of the associate managers attempted to copy store manager George in their management styles. Most of them were abusive, abrasive, and dictatorial in the way that they related to their subordinates.

I remember one associate manager who transferred in from another store. She was a hard worker but was very pleasant. Her people loved her because she was fair and treated them like adults. She did not last six months before George ran her off.

Another result of this management style is that there is no loyalty created in the workforce. If employees are treated poorly, they are not going to do any more work than they have to. They are not going to look for ways to make the business or the organization better. If they are managed by intimidation, they will not feel a sense of their own value to the company. If they don't feel that they are valued, they will only do the minimum amount of work that they can get away with.

Another result of Management by Fear is high turnover. The turnover rate at George's store was extremely high. The average time an associate lasted at the store was about three months. They just could not keep people. I would hear George and his associates talking about it, "Why can't we keep people? We pay more than any other store in the mall."

When another employee would quit, it wasn't unusual to hear an associate manager say, "Well, they just did not want to work." In reality, the person did want to work, but they wanted to work in a place where they were appreciated, treated with respect, and treated fairly. They were willing to take less money to find more peace of mind.

Leadership Take Aways

1. Do you feel that your boss appreciates you?

2. Do you feel like what you do matters?

3. When was the last time a supervisor or manager publicly praised and honored you or one of your peers?

4. Have you ever had a boss who managed by fear? How did you handle it?

Chapter Twenty-Nine

Management by Involvement

Another business that I had the opportunity to observe up close and personal was Walmart. They also hired a number of local police officers to work security there during the overnight shift. They are open twenty-four hours and were having a lot of thefts late at night. Walmart is the largest retailer in the world. It was interesting to see how they "did" management.

What impressed me right away was how visible and approachable the managers were. This included the store manager, as well as all the assistant managers. They did not hide in their offices. Other than the store manager, I am not even sure the assistants had offices. They were almost always on the floor, working with and alongside their subordinates.

One night, a large shipment of goods came in and needed to be put out on the shelves. Big boxes were blocking the aisles. A number of employees were standing around, talking, laughing, and cutting up. There wasn't much work getting done. The night manager walked up. Instead of telling them to get to work, he said, "Hey guys. We need to get this stuff put away. Can you help me?" He then started working, opening the boxes and putting items on shelves. Everyone else joined in.

The manager worked alongside his subordinates for about ten

minutes. He then said, "I have to go check on the rest of the store but I will be back later and see how you are doing. Let me know if you need anything." He then left and the subordinates kept working until the job was finished.

This Walmart manager did three things that I think are worth mentioning. First of all, he told the subordinates what needed to be done. He did it, however, by requesting their help. Secondly, he showed them by example that he expected them to work. He did not just tell them what to do and leave. He worked alongside the workers for a few minutes. The last thing that the manager did was to let them know that he expected the job to be completed. This was done very subtly. He merely said as he left that he would be back to check on them later.

Anytime you compare and contrast two big companies, you are going to be painting with large brush strokes. I'm pretty sure that every manager in George's company is not as bad as he was. If you missed it, I discussed him in the last two chapters, "Management by Fear? Parts One and Two." There are probably some good ones out there. And every Walmart manager is probably not as good as the one I described here.

What these two examples do, however, is provide us with a starting place for evaluating what our own management style is. Our most valuable asset is not our bank account, our buildings, infrastructure, customer base, or our computer system. Our most valuable asset is our people.

On them, we succeed or we fail. They can make us or break us. If we fail to realize this and try and manage by fear, intimidation, or manipulation, we will find that our most talented people will go somewhere else. And who can blame them?

Leadership Take Aways

1. What do you think of the Walmart manager that I just described?

2. Do you think that he was an effective manager?

3. Would you like to work for someone like that?

4. How do you think your subordinates perceive your management style?

5. Does it lean more towards fear or involvement?

Chapter Thirty

How Did Jesus Develop Leaders?

When Jesus started His public ministry, he handpicked a group of men to follow Him. While most people are familiar with the Twelve Disciples, in actuality, Jesus had many more followers than that. The Twelve were later pulled from this much larger group to be the key leaders in carrying Jesus' message to the world after he was gone.

Jesus trained his followers in three ways. First of all, he allowed them to observe him at work. They were with him as he taught and performed miracles. There were occasions after Jesus had taught that his disciples would come to him seeking clarification. He would often break down and dissect what he had just taught the crowd to make sure that his closest followers understood the parable or teaching.

Because Jesus' followers would be expected to perform the same type of works that he had performed, he let them observe him performing many types of miracles, including healings and even raising people from the dead. On almost every occasion, Jesus had his followers with him when he performed these supernatural signs. In some of these instances, he even allowed his disciples to participate in the miracle.

This was the case in the two miraculous feedings. In one case he fed over five thousand people and another time he fed four thousand people. In Mark 6:41, for example, the food was multiplied as Jesus gave it to the disciples and they distributed it to the crowd.

The second way that Jesus trained his followers was that he after they had been with him for awhile watching him work, he sent them out on short ministry trips. These trips were great opportunities for the disciples to get real ministry experience while spreading the Gospel message. After these ministry trips, the disciples reported back to Jesus about all they did. They would then spend time discussing their results and receiving further training from Jesus.

On one occasion, Jesus sent out a large group of seventy-two of his followers out on a ministry trip. They were paired up and sent to some of the villages and cities that Jesus was planning on visiting. When they returned from their trip, they proudly reported that they had been able to cast out evil spirits, just like Jesus. Jesus used this as a teaching point to stress what was really important. "But don't rejoice just because evil spirits obey you; rejoice because your names are registered as citizens of heaven."

The last way that Jesus trained his followers was that he sent his Holy Spirit to live inside them. When Jesus left the earth he sent the Holy Spirit back to indwell his people. Jesus promised that the Holy Spirit would lead his followers into all truth and continue to teach them. This began to take place in the early Church as Christ's followers attempted to do the right things. There was, of course some trial and error but as the early Christians prayed for guidance and then stepped out in faith, the Holy Spirit directed their steps.

One example of this was in Acts fifteen. The Church was faced with a major decision. It was a decision that would affect every succeeding generation of Christians. It involved the question of whether or not non-Jews should be circumcised and required to obey the Jewish law to be considered Christians. After some spirited debate, it was decided to not make it difficult on the non-Jews turning to Christ. They were not required to keep the entire law. Salvation by faith became the understood way for people to become followers of Christ and members of the Church.

James, one of the primary leaders in the early Church wrote a letter to non-Jews explaining the decision. The non-Jews were asked to avoid sexual immorality, idolatry, and asked to observe a few minor dietary restrictions so they could maintain fellowship with their Jewish brothers. James said in the letter, "It seemed good to the Holy Spirit and to us not to place an unnecessary burden on those who are turning to Christ." There was a conscious sense that the leaders of the Church were acting in concert with God's plan.

Thankfully, those who follow Christ still have access to the Holy Spirit. The Church, however, is led by people. The pattern that Jesus left was a Spirit-filled, Spirit-equipped, group of people who continue to learn from their leaders, each other, and the Holy Spirit.

Chapter Thirty-One

The Unprotected City

"A person without self-control is like a city with broken-down walls."

We don't see many cities in America with walls. That is not a common architectural feature today. Cities, however, used to be built with large, thick walls around them to keep the bad guys out and the good guys safe within. The large gate could be opened and closed to limit access to the city. In Brazil, where my wife and I are working, almost every house and every apartment complex are surrounded by a high wall with pointy things or an electric wire on top.

This proverb presents an interesting word picture by putting the character quality of self-control on the same level as the protective wall around a city. It actually makes a lot of sense if you stop and think about it, though. Have you ever seen a co-worker commit career suicide because they could not keep their mouth closed? Or maybe you had a family member that got arrested every few years because they just could not control their drinking or their temper.

I saw it over and over again in my law enforcement career. I probably would not have had a job if people could just exercise self-control. The angry husband who hit his wife, the lady who had one too many drinks at dinner and is now going to try and drive home, the teenage girl who just had to have that expensive shirt and shoplifted it are just a few examples of how a lack of self-control can destroy people.

Self-control is one of those qualities that will make us successful in life. As parents, this must be one of the main things that we try to instill in our children from a young age. They may not enjoy it at the time but they will thank us for it later. As adults, we never get past the need to stay disciplined and self-controlled in our lives. How many marriages have been destroyed, careers flushed down the toilets, and lives ended early because of a lack of self-control?

By developing the quality of self-control in our lives, we are raising a wall of protection around ourselves. By teaching our children how to control themselves, we are helping to build that wall around them. Self-control will help all of us in every area of life.

Leadership Take Aways

1. How is your self-control?

2. Has a lack of self-control ever hurt you?

3. As a leader, do you see this as an area that is easy to ignore?

4. What kind of damage can a leader do if they neglect this important area?

Chapter Thirty-Two

Half Full or Half Empty?

The optimists see the glass and say, "It is half full."

The pessimists see the glass and say, "It is half empty."

The faith person sees the glass and says, "It is completely full."

The faith person understands that the glass contains 50% water and 50% air. It is 100% full. The faith person has learned the power of seeing the invisible.

We can't do the impossible until we see the invisible. That only will happen when we connect our natural to God's supernatural through the power of faith.

"What is faith? It is the confident assurance that what we hope for is going to happen. It is the evidence of things we cannot yet see." (Hebrews 11:1)

What kind of leader are you?

Are you a half full, half empty, or completely full kind of leader?

Are you a half full or a half empty leader?

What would it take to make you a leader who sees the invisible?

Do you see possibilities where others see problems?

Chapter Thirty-Three

Little Distractions or Big Dreams?

"Don't be on your deathbed someday, having squandered your one chance at life, full of regret because you pursued little distractions instead of big dreams." Derek Stivers

Life is full of these "little distractions" that keep us from following our dreams. There are many days that I find myself forgetting about my Big Dream. I'm too busy doing other stuff that one has to do to survive: working, answering e-mails, paying bills, getting the oil changed in the car, returning phone calls. What was that Big Dream that I used to have?

What about you? Only you know what your Big Dream is. It is that thing that you would love to do, if it weren't for all the little distractions. I think managing our distractions is a part of life. It is a natural tension brought on by doing what we have to do versus what we really want to be do.

So what is the answer? Here is a suggestion that has helped me. Why don't you commit to doing something every day that is going to take you a little closer to your Dream? It might mean reading a book about starting a business. It might mean taking one college course at a time on-line. It might mean getting a second job to make the extra money you are going to need to purchase that house you want.

What is one thing that you can do today to take you a little closer to where you want to be? Who knows, you might just wake up one day and see that your Big Dream is much closer than you thought!

Chapter Thirty-Four

Getting Out of the Ditch

Have you ever felt that you were stuck in your life? There were a lot of cars stuck in ditches all around Atlanta last year during the annual snow and ice storm. Atlanta does not get much snow and ice, but what we do get creates chaos for so many people. Thankfully, for most of these stuck motorists, a call to a tow truck and a hundred dollars later, they were back on the road.

It is a little more complicated to get your life unstuck, though. None of us like living in a rut. Living there leads to frustration, depression, and apathy. The reason that most of us get stuck is that we lose momentum in our lives. We feel that we have gone as far as we can go in our profession, our relationships have grown stale, or we don't feel that we are growing in our personal lives.

I heard Andy Stanley comment on a recent podcast that, "Change creates momentum." I have found that making changes, even small changes in my life, can provide a fresh perspective and generate some momentum. With a car that is stuck in the mud, it often just takes a little bit of forward momentum to get it out of the mud and moving again.

What are some things that we can change to generate some fresh momentum?

1. Change your workout routine. Try some new machines or exercises. Buy a few sessions with a personal trainer. If you don't have a workout routine, start one.

2. Instead of listening to music on the way to work, listen to a book on CD or a podcast. Why not use your commute as a time to learn something new?

3. Do something different at work. I realize that this not always possible. If the opportunity is there, however, look for new ways to do your job, or talk to your boss about some additional responsibilities.

4. Meet some new people. Being around the same people all the time might give us a sense of security, but making new friends can help give us a fresh perspective and a push to get us out of that rut.

Leadership Take Aways

1. Can you think of any other ways to get unstuck?

2. What did you do the last time you found yourself in a rut?

Chapter Thirty-Five

Good Decisions = A Good Life

"Good planning and hard work lead to prosperity." Solomon

In the same way that bad decisions set us up for failure, so good decisions and good life planning lead to success. Unfortunately, too many of us go through life with no plan other than to make it to Friday. If that is the extent of our vision, we should not be surprised that life is a struggle for us. Maybe you have heard these questions before:

"Why did they get promoted? I have worked here longer than they have." Maybe it is because they are at work early, stay late, work hard, and don't criticize their boss?

"Why do they have such a good marriage?" Maybe because they work really hard at it, know how to resolve conflict, and are both going in the same direction in life?

"Why did their kids turn out so good?" Maybe because they started molding their will at an early age and have made raising their children a top priority of their lives?

"Why are they being blessed financially?" Maybe because they are generous people who understand the power of giving, saving, and minimizing their debt?

"Why are their employees always in a good mood?" Maybe because she treats them like adults, creates a positive environment to work in, and does not micromanage them?

Leadership Take Aways

1. Are you happy with where you are at in life?

2. How are your life planning skills?

3. Where do you see room for improvement?

Chapter Thirty-Six

A Season of Change- Setting Goals

Goal setting is a vital skill for anyone to master if they are going to succeed in life. Our goals will often determine our failure or our success. In setting goals for our lives, career, family, finances, etc., remember that your goals should be SMART:

1. Specific.

A general goal would be to, "Get out of debt." A specific goal would be to, "Pay off one credit card." We have a much better chance of reaching our goals if they are specific. A general goal could be to, "Lose weight." A specific goal would be to, "Lose ten pounds," or to, "Drop two pants sizes."

2. Measurable.

If someone wants to get in shape physically in the coming year, a measurable goal could be to, "Lose ten pounds by March," or to, "Reduce my body fat percentage by five points by my next birthday." If you can measure your progress, there will be no question about when the goal is met.

3. Attainable.

A goal is attainable when I am willing to take the steps that are needed to make it happen. Am I willing to pay the price? Losing ten pounds is only attainable if I am determined to start an exercise regimen and watch my diet. Paying off one credit card this year is only attainable if you are willing to become more disciplined in your spending habits.

4. Realistic.

If your goal is, "To earn $100,000 this year," that is probably not very realistic if you only earn minimum wage and just work thirty hours a week. It might be more realistic to look at what you earned last year, and then consider how much you could make if you worked more hours, got a second job, or were able to get promoted in your current job. Everybody's reality is going to be different. What is actually going to work for you?

5. Timely.

What is your time frame for reaching your goal? A year is a great time frame to work within. You can break the year down into months, quarters, or thirds depending on what you want to accomplish. When you set a date that you want to accomplish your goal by, you establish a deadline in your subconscious that helps push you towards it. When you write it down, the goal actually becomes real. Until you put your goal on paper or on the computer screen it is not really real.

Leadership Take Aways

1. Do you have your goals written down somewhere that you can see them regularly?

2. Do you update your goals throughout the year?

3. How intentional are you are setting and then accomplishing goals?

Chapter Thirty-Seven

A Season of Change- Writing it Down

"Did you write your goals today? Remember, goals without action are like smoke in the air. They just dissipate, never becoming reality."

Writing your goals down is the first action step towards seeing them become reality. If we don't write them down, it is unlikely that we will follow through and do our part to see these goals fulfilled. Putting a goal on paper (or typing them onto a computer screen) is the first tangible step that we can make to put ourselves in the proper frame of mind to work towards a specific goal. Until we write them down, our goals do not become real to us.

After you have written your goals down, the next step is to put them somewhere that you can see them daily. It might be on your bathroom mirror or for some it could even be sticking them on your refrigerator. I keep my list in the front of my Bible. Wherever you put your list of goals, it needs to be something that you look at, pray over, and meditate on daily.

Begin to visualize what your life will look like after the goal is fulfilled. Imagine hearing someone compliment you on how good you look after losing twenty pounds. Imagine the freedom you will feel after you get a credit card paid off. This is not wasted daydreaming! If you can't see the goal fulfilled in your imagination first, it is not likely that you will follow through and do what needs to be done to bring it to pass.

Thinking about our goals is just not enough. We need to put them on paper or the computer screen. There is something powerful that happens when we actually write that goal down. This simple act is often one of the most important steps to seeing that goal fulfilled.

Leadership Take Aways

1. Do you write your goals down?

2. If you do write them down, how often do you review them?

3. How could creating better goals and writing them down help you in the next year?

Chapter Thirty-Eight

Is There Ever a Perfect Time?

"Farmers who wait for perfect weather never plant. If they watch every cloud, they never harvest."

Have you ever fallen into the trap of thinking:

"This is not really a good time to start a business."

"I need to make a little more money before we can get married."

"We can't afford to have children."

"I don't have the time to write that book."

"I'll wait for a better time to invite them to church."

Timing in life is important, but it is not that important. Doing something is better than doing nothing. There is seldom the "perfect" moment to act.

Yes, it is nice when the stars line up, and everything falls into place. If I spend my life waiting for that, though, I am not going to accomplish much. Farmers plant their seed, even if the weather looks bad. A partial crop is better than no crop.

Is there something that you are waiting to do?

What is it that is holding you back?

Chapter Thirty-Nine

Leadership Equals Clarity

There are so many definitions for leadership. Imparting vision, exerting influence, providing direction, guiding a group toward goals, etc., are all good definitions. One definition of leadership that is not talked about as much though, is that leaders provide clarity.

We can give direction, vision and exert influence but without clarity, though, our people are just going to be confused. In a very real sense, as leaders we should be removing the clutter so that our people can do their jobs. Leaders clear a path through the jungle.

There is nothing better than meeting with the boss, CEO, or pastor and leaving with clarity. We know where we are going and how we are going to get there. We know what everyone's roles are and what is required of us. There is no confusion. The leader has made things clear.

Leadership Take Aways

1. Do you feel that as a leader, you make things clear for your people?

2. Have you worked for a leader that did not make things as clear as they needed to be?

4. How can you bring more clarity to your organization?

Chapter Forty

The Why of Leadership

"Effective leaders do more than call on people to perform a given task out of duty or responsibility, though there's a place for duty and responsibility. They know that people are more than cogs in a wheel or numbers on a stat sheet. They know that meaning moves people. Effective leaders help people understand the why behind the what, where, how, and when." Daniel Allen, Jr., from *Summoned: Stepping Up to Live and Lead with Jesus*

Managers provide the "what." They tell us what needs to be

done. Managers also tell us the where, the how, and the when of the job. These are all good and important things for every organization. Our people have to know the what, where, how, and when. These things provide the guidelines for how every organization operates.

Leaders provide the "why." The "why" gives meaning to everything that we do. If we do not understand why we are doing what we are doing, we do not really understand the mission of our organization. Everyone should know what the mission is if we expect to be successful. From the CEO or the Senior Pastor to the entry level new hire or the newest volunteer, everyone should understand the "why" so they can all be a part of fulfilling the mission.

Leadership Take Aways

1. Do you understand the why of your job?

2. If you are a leader, how do you communicate the why to your team?

Chapter Forty-One

Lessons Learned from Bad Bosses

In my long career in Law Enforcement, I was privileged to be able to work for some great supervisors and leaders. I also had my share of terrible bosses. While I learned so much from the good bosses, I also picked up a lot of leadership take aways from the bad ones. Here are a few of the leadership lessons that I learned from some bad bosses.

1. Don't make a decision.

Be indecisive as long as you can under the guise of trying to get as much information as you can. When a subordinate tries get you make a decision, remind them that there is a lot at stake and you need to consider every possibility before deciding on the issue. Hopefully, the deadline will pass and you can blame the subordinate for not giving you enough information to start with. If you don't make a decision, then you can be assured you will not make the wrong decision.

2. Have a different personality every day.

Keep your people guessing as to whether Happy Boss, Angry Boss, Depressed Boss, or Driven Boss is going to show up. Exhibiting a different personality every day is a great way to keep your people in line and drive them to need therapy.

3. Dominate every conversation.

If one of your employees shares one of their accomplishments, make sure you one-up them with one of your spectacular accomplishments. We can not have our subordinates outshining us. Practice this phrase in front of a mirror, "That is nothing. One time I... INSERT YOUR OWN STORY HERE."

4. When you give assignments, make sure you tell your subordinate exactly how to do the job, down to the most minuscule detail.

Even if they think they have a better way to do it, make sure they do it just the way that you would. We can't have our people thinking too much for themselves. Learning how to micromanage is an art form that every bad boss must master.

5. Don't learn anything about your subordinate's personal lives.

It is not important for you to know if they are married or have kids to get the most out of them at work. If you get to know them, you might actually begin to care about them. How unprofessional would that be! The last thing we would want to do is actually get to know the people that work for us.

6. Take credit for your subordinate's work.

If your team accomplishes their sales goal, make sure you tell your boss how it was your strategy and your motivational speeches that made it happen. Of course, if your team misses their goal, make sure you let your boss know what a bunch of worthless people you have working for you.

7. If you have to correct or coach one of your team members, make sure you do it in public so that everyone can hear it.

Sure, it might be a little embarrassing for that person, but if everyone else on the team hears it, they are less likely to make the same mistake. Never miss a chance to correct someone who is not doing things exactly the way that you would. A little public humiliation will serve to keep everyone in line.

What are some other lessons that you have learned from working for a bad boss

Chapter Forty-Two

Owning It

"Then David said to Abiathar, "That day, when Doeg the Edomite was there, I knew he would be sure to tell Saul. I am responsible for the death of your whole family." (1 Samuel 22:22)

"Then David said to Nathan, "I have sinned against the Lord." Nathan replied, "The Lord has taken away your sin. You are not going to die." (2 Samuel 12:13)

The man who we know as King David made a lot of mistakes. Of course, his biggest sins were murder and adultery. Why is it, though, that we still read his Psalms and celebrate his legacy as Israel's greatest king? Why is it that Jesus was often referred to as "the Son of David," and the one who would receive "the throne of his father David?"

One of the reasons for his legacy was the fact that David was a man who knew how to take responsibility for his actions. When he sinned spectacularly and was confronted about it, he did not try and excuse himself or blame someone else. He owned his sin, he accepted responsibility, and he took whatever discipline that came his way.

By way of contrast, the man who David replaced as Israel's king, King Saul, was a man who never accepted responsibility for his sins and mistakes. Instead, he looked for others to blame. Look at these examples:

"What have you done?" asked Samuel. Saul replied, "When I saw that the men were scattering, and that you did not come at the set time, and that the Philistines were assembling at Mikmash, I thought, 'Now the Philistines will come down against me at Gilgal, and I have not sought the Lord's favor.' So I felt compelled to offer the burnt offering." "You have done a foolish thing," Samuel said. "You have not kept the command the Lord your God gave you; if you had, he would have established your kingdom over Israel for all time. But now your kingdom will not endure; the Lord has sought out a man after his own heart and appointed him ruler of his people, because you have not kept the Lord's command." (1 Samuel 13:11-14)

On another occasion, we read, "But Samuel said, "What then is this bleating of sheep in my ears? What is this lowing of cattle that I hear?" Saul answered, "The soldiers brought them from the Amalekites; they spared the best of the sheep and cattle to sacrifice to the Lord your God, but we totally destroyed the rest." (1 Samuel 15:14-15)

Saul sinned and sinned badly on numerous occasions. He, however, never took ownership of what he had done. In almost every case, he looked for someone else was to blame. It was never his fault. Saul refused to accept responsibility.

One of the hallmarks of strong leadership is a willingness to accept responsibility and to admit when we have done wrong. Leaders who can do this earn the respect and the deep loyalty of their followers. No one expects perfect leaders. We do expect the leader to own it when he or she gets it wrong.

Leadership Take Aways

1. Do you have trouble owning it?

2. Do you ever look for someone else to blame?

3. When a leader owns a mistake, how does that make you feel about them?

Chapter Forty-Three

Always Learning

"Our level of teachability is the ultimate level of our growth."

One of the things that I have noticed about the best leaders that I have been around is that they are all life-long learners. They never seem to think that they know enough. They are always reading, listening, and educating themselves.

Knowledge is power. Knowing how to use and apply that knowledge is wisdom. There has never been a better time to be a leader. There are resources available today that leaders in previous generations would have loved to have.

While reading, listening to podcasts, and going to conferences are all excellent ways to improve ourselves, they never replace the importance of allowing someone to have input into our lives. Having a mentor, coach, or just a good friend who is a little further down the road than we are is vital. Who are you allowing to help you go to the next level?

Let's take advantage of every opportunity to get better. Let's take advantage of every opportunity to stretch ourselves. Our people deserve the best leadership that we can give them!

What are you doing to develop your leadership skills?

Chapter Forty-Four

Losing it All

> "But when King Uzziah had become powerful, he also became proud, which led to his downfall..." (2 Chronicles 26:16)

> "King Jotham became powerful because he was careful to live in obedience to the Lord his God." (2 Chronicles 27:6)

Uzziah was one of the longest reigning and most successful kings in Judah's history. His success, however, also led to his downfall. His pride caused him to think that he was above the law.

God's laws applied to everyone but him. King Uzziah went into the temple and attempted to to do what only the priest was supposed to do.

When the High Priest and eighty other priests confronted Uzziah, the king became furious. Who were they to tell him what he could and could not do? God's judgment was quick and severe. King Uzziah contracted leprosy and spent his last days isolated and alone. His son, Jotham, was given the throne of his father. It was rare to crown the son king while the father was still alive but Uzziah's leprosy kept him out of public life until his death.

Jotham was a wise young man and became a very good king. An important component of wisdom is being able to learn from someone else's successes and from their mistakes. King Jotham learned much from his father, both good and bad.

"Jotham did what was pleasing in the Lord's sight. He did everything his father, Uzziah, had done, except that Jotham did not sin by entering the Temple of the Lord." (2 Chronicles 27:2) King Jotham understood his role and responsibilities as the king and did not try to step over the limits of his own God-given authority.

Success can be a dangerous thing. We all want it. We all seek it. We have to be so careful, though, when we attain it. Success brings it's own set of temptations. If we allow success to change us we are headed for a fall. Pride and arrogance have caused more leaders to fall than anything else.

Jotham provides a great example for us. He had watched his father. He saw what had worked and what did not. King Jotham avoided the mistakes that his father made but also applied the good things that he learned from Uzziah.

Charisma and talent might very well get someone into a leadership position. Humility and teachability, however, are going to keep them there for the long haul. If you are interested in reading more about this important aspect of leadership, check out Dr. Tim Irwin's incredible book *Derailed: Five Lessons Learned from Catastrophic Failures of Leadership*.

This book provides some excellent modern day case studies of men and women CEO's, who like Uzziah, thought that the rules did not apply to them. It is a fascinating and sobering book. Dr. Irwin reminds us that success has caused more leaders to fall than failure ever has.

Have you ever struggled with success?

Chapter Forty-Five

How Healthy is Your Team?

"Since God chose you to be the holy people whom he loves, you must clothe yourselves with tenderhearted mercy, kindness, humility, gentleness, and patience. You must make allowance for each other's faults and forgive the person who offends you. Remember, the Lord forgave you, so you must forgive others. And the most important piece of clothing you must wear is love. Love is what binds us all together in perfect harmony."
(Colossians 3:12-14)

It is no secret that the health of our leadership team is what will ultimately determine the health of our organization. An unhealthy team will eventually affect the entire church, company, or organization. What are some of the things that we can do to keep our team healthy?

1. Support your leaders.

This sounds so basic, yet how often do you hear people criticizing and berating those who are over us? We should always speak well of our leaders in public. If we criticize and gossip, we are giving everyone else in the organization permission to do the same thing. If we have disagreements, they should be handled behind closed doors, not in public.

Another way that we can support our leaders is to give them positive feedback. Just because they are the boss does not mean that they do not need encouragement. Encouragement is oxygen for the soul and those over us need it like everyone else.

Another aspect of supporting our leaders is that we need to give them grace. As the passage above says, "You must make allowance for each other's faults…" Everyone has a bad day, even the boss. Let's extend the same grace to them that we would like to have extended to us.

2. Support your fellow team-members.

As a team we have to look out for each other. This does not mean that we have to all be best friends. Of course, it helps if we are friends and actually like each other. Team dynamics, though, often can create tension in the relationships on the team.

One of the ways that we can support our team-members is by speaking well of them in public. It is always easy to criticize someone that we do not like or agree with. By having a default setting of always speaking positively of our co-workers and teammates, we are presenting a unified front to the rest of the organization. If we have a problem with a co-worker, we should be mature enough to confront them instead of gossiping about them.

Encouraging our fellow team-members is another way that we can support them. It can be difficult sometimes to encourage a co-worker's accomplishments, especially if we feel that we are in competition with them. Encouragement, however, helps us to create a positive atmosphere on our team. Everyone wants to work in this kind of atmosphere. If we can create a culture of celebrating each other's successes, we are going a long way to creating a healthy team and ultimately, a healthy organization.

Another way that we show support for our co-workers is by giving them grace. As we said above, everyone can have a bad day. If we can learn how to extend the grace that we would like to receive when we are having a bad day, things will go much smoother.

3. Remember your mission.

Why are we there? Our organizational mission should define everything that we do as a team. Everyone on the team should be clear on the leader's vision and where the organization is going. It is good to revisit the vision from time-to-time to keep everyone focused on what we are supposed to be doing. A strong sense of mission will go a long way to creating a strong sense of unity among our team.

What other things would you add to the list for keeping your team healthy?

Chapter Forty-Six

Keys to Reading More

Leaders are readers.

Most of us have heard this statement and even agree with it but life has a way of interfering with what we know we should do. It sounds like a great New Year's Resolution or goal to read more books but how can we sustain the habit throughout the year? I want to give you a few tips that can help you make reading a bigger part of your life.

For the last thirty years, I have consistently read fifty to sixty books a year. For many people that sounds like a lot of books! But how would you like to have a goal of reading one book a month? Reading twelve books a years is a great goal to have.

So, how can you reach this milestone?

1. Set aside a few minutes each day for reading.

Where can you carve out a few minutes to read a good book? Maybe you could read on your lunch break. Of course, this would mean not checking your Facebook or Instagram accounts but twenty minutes of reading at lunch would probably translate to reading at least one book a month.

Some people like to read at night before going to bed. If you do this, I would suggest turning the TV off a few minutes early and reading while you are still somewhat awake. Reading right before you go to sleep is not the best idea.

If you go to the gym, your cardio time on the treadmill or stationary bike can be a great time to read a good book. Audio books are also excellent to listen to while you are working out or doing your cardio. Many people listen to audio books while they are walking their dog.

2. Take advantage of your commute.

My home city in the United States is Atlanta, Georgia. The average worker in Atlanta has a commute of forty minutes. What do you do on your commute besides fuming at the traffic and the bad drivers around you? What if you used that time to listen to audio books? With a thirty to forty minute commute one way, you could probably listen to three or four books a month. Public libraries have hundreds of audio books that you can check out for free. Take advantage of them!

3. Read what interests you.

This sounds so basic but too often we can fall into the trap of thinking we need to read things that are "good" for us. This is not a bad thing but if we are not in the habit of reading at all, it is probably best that we get into the habit by reading things that we enjoy. Self-help books, leadership books, and financial planning books are all great. At the same time, however, reading good fiction stimulates our minds and can help us to become more creative. Read what you enjoy!

4. Talk to others about what you are reading.

What are you learning from your reading? I find that when I talk to a friend about a book that we have both read or are reading, it helps me to process the information better. Book Clubs are great opportunities to meet new people and discuss great books. There are even on-line communities that talk about books. You could even start your own group with two or three friends that all want to b better themselves.

What is holding you back from becoming a more consistent reader?

Chapter Forty-Seven

Rabbi Jesus and His Band of Merry Men

"One day as Jesus was walking along the shores of the Sea of Galilee, he saw Simon and his brother, Andrew, fishing with a net, for they were commercial fishermen. Jesus called out to them, "Come, be my disciples, and I will show you how to fish for people!" And they left their nets at once and went with him. A little farther up the shore Jesus saw Zebedee's sons, James and John, in a boat mending their nets. He called them, too, and immediately they left their father, Zebedee, in the boat with the hired men and went with him."

"As Jesus was going down the road, he saw Matthew sitting at his tax-collection booth. "Come, be my disciple," Jesus said to him. So Matthew got up and followed him."

In his day, Jesus wasn't the only Jewish teacher in the land. There were many other rabbis with disciples. There are, however, some notable differences in the way that Jesus did things. As leaders, what can we learn from Jesus' relationship with his disciples?

1. Traditionally, the student picked his rabbi.

The student would shop around until he found a teacher that he felt comfortable with. Jesus, however, went out and handpicked His followers. The disciples did not pick Jesus. He picked them. Isn't it interesting the kind of people he chose as his followers? He could have picked some bright young religious students but instead, he chose people out of different segments of society: fishermen, a tax collector, a revolutionary, probably some farmers, etc.

LEADERSHIP PRINCIPLE: We are always on the lookout for people that have leadership potential. This will often mean giving untried people a chance and giving responsibility to people to see how they handle it.

2. Traditionally, the Torah or Law was what stood at the center of the relationship between the rabbi and his disciples.

Jesus made it clear to his disciples that he was at the center of their relationship. Instead of teaching them the Law, Jesus taught them about the Kingdom of God. He even reduced the Law down to its most basic components: Love God with all your heart and love your neighbor as you love yourself. In Mark, Jesus' teaching to his disciples is also focused on preparing them for His death. "The shadow of the cross falls ever more darkly" as the gospel continues. Much of Jesus' ministry was to equip his followers so that they could keep going when he was gone.

LEADERSHIP PRINCIPLE: We bring the Kingdom of God into every situation of our lives. We bring the Kingdom to the people that we pastor in church, at our jobs, and in our neighborhoods. God's will is that His Kingdom be established on earth as it is in heaven.

3. Traditionally, the relationship between the rabbi and his followers was that of a master/student type.

There was a clear delineation of power. The relationship that Jesus had with His disciples was much deeper. He called them "friends." This unique relationship affected how Jesus' disciples learned.

Traditional rabbis taught their followers in a traditional way- lecture, memorization, study, etc. Jesus' disciples learned by watching Him. They watched Jesus in everyday contact with real people in real situations. A great example of this was in Jesus raising little the girl from the dead and then, later, Peter raising Dorcas from the dead in the Acts of the Apostles. Peter does what he saw Jesus do.

LEADERSHIP PRINCIPLE: People learn how to live and be successful by watching us. In the arena of service in the church, people learn more by watching than they do by us telling them. Our example is the most important way that we teach others.

4. The rabbinical schools eventually evolved into exclusive groups of disciples.

The Pharisees, Sadducees and their disciples loved to flaunt their knowledge and used their positions to gain prestige and power over others. Jesus, however, called His followers to be servants, to endure persecution, and to be the salt and light of the world. He said, "You know that the rulers in this world lord it over their people, and officials flaunt their authority over those under them. But among you it will be different. Whoever wants to be a leader among you must be your servant, and whoever wants to be first among you must be the slave of everyone else. For even the Son of Man came not to be served but to serve others and to give his life as a ransom for many." (Mark 10: 42-45)

Learning how to serve is a prerequisite for true Kingdom leadership and for true success in life. It is unlikely that any other rabbi would have ever considered washing his student's feet. Jesus turned social norms upside down by kneeling on the floor, taking on the role of a servant, and washing his follower's feet.

LEADERSHIP PRINCIPLE: The higher up the leadership ladder we go only increases the amount that we are required to serve. Do you want to be a leader? Develop a servant's heart. Leadership flows out of service.

5. The call of Jesus to His disciples went far beyond what the other rabbis expected of their disciples.

The implication was strong that at some point, the disciples could expect to lose their lives in their service of Jesus. No other rabbi would ever teach this way or require this depth of a commitment from their followers. The idea of giving their lives in the service of their rabbi would never have even entered their minds. For Jesus' followers, however, the cost of following him was great, but the reward was even greater.

LEADERSHIP PRINCIPLE: Let's not be afraid to challenge people. It's easy as leaders to fall into the trap of catering to peoples' comfort zones. Be sensitive to the Holy Spirit and people's needs but don't hesitate to call them "higher up and further in" as C. S. Lewis would

Chapter Forty-Eight

Creating Culture

Every organization has a particular culture. That culture can be created by default (doing nothing) or can be created intentionally by the leaders. It has been said that leaders are social architects. If this is true, creating and programming an organization's culture is an important leadership role.

Culture that is created by default is usually not healthy. When we create culture, however, we can put the values that we want into the organization's DNA. Our values will always shape our culture.

Here are three ways that we can create the culture that we want in our organizations:

1. We talk about it.

Check out 2 Timothy 3:10-11 and Philippians 3:1. We never get tired of talking about what is important. In meetings, sermons, conversations, emails, Facebook posts, website, and other social media, we constantly talk about the things that are important and make up our culture.

Leaders especially have to talk about the type of culture that they want to see in the business, organization, or church. There should never be a mystery about what our values are and what we want the organization to look like. It is not a secret. We want everyone to know how want the organization to look, act, and feel. When you think you have talked about culture enough, you are just getting started.

2. We live it.

The power of example is seen over and over again in the life of the Apostle Paul. He wrote to his friends in Philippi, "Imitate me as I follow Christ." (Philippians. 4:9) Our people will learn much more by watching us than by just listening to what we say. Our example is powerful and we must never forget that our employees, volunteers, and members are watching us closely. If we live what we say, they will probably help us in creating and perpetuating the kind of culture that we want.

3. We praise others who practice our values.

Look at 1 Corinthians 16:15-18. Publicly honoring those who are living out our values is so important. When we publicly praise those who are practicing our values, we are reinforcing, in a powerful way, what we want to see practiced. There is not much more powerful than when we honor someone in front of their peers and hold them up as an example. This will inspire the same kind of behavior in others.

What are some other ways that we can create the right kind of culture?

Chapter Forty-Nine

The Importance of Wisdom

"Getting wisdom is the wisest thing you can do! And whatever else you do, develop good judgment." (Proverbs 4:7)

We are fortunate to live in a time in which knowledge is literally at our fingertips. Google can provide the answer to almost any question in just seconds. Rather than having to spend hours at a library looking for an answer, we can find what we want to know almost instantly.

Knowledge, however, is very different from wisdom. Knowledge is important and some have even said that knowledge is power. In reality, though, knowledge is power only when we know how to use it. That is where wisdom comes in.

How can we develop and increase our level of wisdom? One of the primary ways is by learning how to be teachable. While knowledge can be gained almost instantly, that alone does not translate into wisdom. A person who is teachable, however, will gain not only knowledge, but also how to apply that knowledge.

I think that there are three factors that help us stay teachable:

1. Humility.

Realizing that we do not have all the answers is an important first step to becoming wise. Even understanding that we often do not even know the right questions to ask is a key to gaining wisdom. Pride and wisdom cancel each other out. I have never met a wise person who was also arrogant.

2. Always learning.

The wisest people that I know are always learning. They are always reading, always taking classes, and always asking questions. They not only want to expand their base of knowledge, they want to learn how to apply that knowledge correctly.

3. Willing to learn from anyone.

Wise people learn from everyone they meet. They understand that anyone might have something to teach them. They are always willing to lay their ego or position aside to learn something new. They are never afraid to look foolish in their quest to become wise.

What other factors do you think lead to someone becoming wise?

Chapter Fifty

Tips for Making a Major Life Change

In 2012, my wife, Annie, and I made a major life change. We left our comfortable home in Atlanta, Georgia. We left our adult daughters, our parents, our friends and an incredible church and moved to Curitiba, Brazil to work with our C3 Churches here. So many of our friends have remarked, "How can you do that? I could never take that kind of a step of faith."

Obviously, a decision to move to another continent is not one to be taken lightly. At the same time, changing jobs, starting a business, getting married, deciding to have children, or buying a second house as an investment property are not decisions that one should take lightly, either. What are some things that need to be considered before someone makes a major life change?

1. Prayer.

For those of us who would say that we are Christians, prayer is the first place to start for any major decision. There is a verse in the Proverbs that says, "Seek his will in all you do, and he will direct your paths." Prayer aligns our hearts, our desires, and our motives with God's will.

When the opportunity came for Annie and I to work with the C3 Churches in Brazil, we spent much time praying for God's guidance. Was this what God wanted? As we sensed that this was what we were supposed to do, the sense of uncertainty was replaced by a sense of peace.

Prayer must not, however, become an excuse for not taking action. At some point, we have to act. God's guidance usually comes as we take that first step. We ask God for His direction and then step towards where we sense Him leading. Our pastor often said, "You move and then God moves." Faith is exercised as we trust him to guide us as we move.

2. Counsel.

No major life change should be undertaken without getting some good advice and counsel. This doesn't mean that we run it by a few of our mates at the gym and get their input. Good counsel means that we go to someone who is a little further down the road of life than we are. This might be our pastor, small group leader, our boss at work, or maybe even our parents.

At every step of the way, Annie and I stayed in close contact with our pastors as we made our decision to move to Brazil. The counsel and advice that they provided was incredible and very helpful. If we are going to get counsel, it is important that we take it seriously. God puts leaders in our lives to help us make the right decisions. Ignoring good counsel can be very dangerous!

3. Timing.

What season of life are you in? Starting your own business might sound like a great idea. You would get to leave the job that you hate and do what you are passionate about. However, if you are carrying significant credit card debt and/or student loans, this is probably not the time to launch out on your own. Instead, developing a plan to get out of debt might be the road that takes you to the place where you can start your business in a few years.

For Annie and I, our season of life contributed to our decision to move to South America. I had recently retired after almost thirty years as a police officer. Our daughters were both grown and married. This was the perfect time for us to make a major life change.

4. Act.

What major life change are you contemplating? So many people have big dreams that they are scared to act on. Don't let fear stop you from making that decision or working towards it. Remember, God's will is often just beyond your comfort zone. Taking that first step is often the hardest step but if you never act, you will always be wondering about what might have been.

Maybe you are not at a place in your life where you can make the big life change that you envision. Do not let that stop you from moving towards your goal! Getting out of debt, going back to school, or starting your business while keeping your full-time job are all good, concrete steps that can move you closer to seeing your dreams come true.

Leadership Take Aways

1. Are you contemplating a major life change?

2. What is one step that you can take today that will bring you closer to making a good decision?

3. What smaller steps can you take to get you where you want to go?

Additional Books by David Spell

1. Peter and Paul in Acts
2. Miracles in Mark
3. New Testament Snapshots
4. Reflections on the Resurrection
5. Street Cop
6. Street Cop II: Reloaded
7. When the Future Ended
8. The Darkest Part of the Night
9. When the Stars Fell From the Sky

All books are available at Amazon.com or at DavidSpell.com.

About the Author

David Spell is a leadership coach, Bible scholar, pastor, and missionary. He taught for many years at the C3 School of Ministry in Atlanta, Georgia. He and Annie served from 2012- 2017 as missionaries in Brazil, where David was the Executive Pastor for C3 Church Curitiba. Now, they are part of the pastoral team at C3 Church in Atlanta, Georgia. David's other books are available at DavidSpell.com where he writes about a variety of topics. Make sure you subscribe so you don't miss a single issue!

www.ingramcontent.com/pod-product-compliance
Lightning Source LLC
Chambersburg PA
CBHW031420210526
45464CB00005B/1973